Written by C. J. McDonald
Designed by Brie Nagy

an imprint of

SCHOLASTIC
scholastic.com

10 9 8 7 6 5 4 3 2 1
ISBN: 978-1-338-64215-5
Made in Guangzhou, China

TABLE OF CONTENTS

THE MOST FEARSOME JAWS ON EARTH

With rows upon rows of flesh-tearing teeth, the shark is the largest predator in the ocean. Just the mention of sharks can strike fear in the bravest heart.

Forget the fact you're more likely to be hit by lightning than attacked by a shark. Forget the fact a tiny mosquito is actually more deadly to humans than sharks. It's not about the numbers. It's about *those jaws*.

Truth is, only about 30 of the 400 known types of sharks have been known to attack people. We're not even close to being their favorite food. But with jaws packed with 3,000 teeth at any given time, sharks have earned their fearsome reputation. That said, these fierce animals have a necessary place in the ecosystem, and they deserve our respect—from a distance!

AN OVERSTATED SENSE OF SMELL

Some people say a shark can smell a drop of blood from a mile away. But they give sharks too much credit. At best, sharks can sniff out a drop of blood in a small swimming pool.

THE TOOTH FAIRY WOULD GO BROKE

These carnivorous fish are born with a full set of teeth so they can immediately begin hunting. They can lose up to 100 teeth in a single day and will have tens of thousands of teeth over the course of their lives.

CHEW ON THIS

We use our teeth for biting, chewing, and grinding. Sharks use their teeth for grabbing and tearing apart prey.' That said, sharks' teeth aren't any stronger than human teeth. They're just sharper and more plentiful—as in a lot sharper and a lot more plentiful!

CAVITY-FREE TOOTH FACTORIES

Sharks' mouths have been described as tooth factories. Back rows of smaller teeth grow and eventually replace the front rows of larger teeth. They may fall out, but they never rot. That's because each tooth is naturally covered with fluoride. No toothpaste or dentist needed!

THE BIGGEST JAWS OF ALL

The jaws of the ancient megalodon shark were 7 ft. (2.1 m) tall and 6 ft. (1.8 m) wide with a bite force five times that of a *Tyrannosaurus rex*! This sea monster was big enough to make lunch of whales.

THE AMPULLAE OF LORENZINI

Sharks have thousands of special receptors on their heads that allow them to detect electrical fields from other animals, an added aid when hunting in dark waters.

YOU'RE NOT ON THE MENU

Most sharks eat small fish and invertebrates. Some eat larger marine animals, such as seals and sea lions. No matter how afraid you are of sharks, they're typically more afraid of you. Only about 66 shark attacks happen worldwide each year. If they bite someone, it's usually accidental.

MADE FOR SPEED

Sharks have skeletons made of lightweight cartilage. They're able to swim 25 mph (40.2 kph)—achieving bursts of 35 mph (56.3 kph)—by swinging their powerful tails from side to side.

FRILLED SHARK

CHLAMYDOSELACHUS ANGUINEUS

A LIVING FOSSIL

Scientists refer to the frilled shark as a living fossil because it looks like something out of prehistoric times. Unlike other sharks, it doesn't have five rows of teeth. Oh, no. It has 25 rows of them! Its bright-white teeth act as a lure for its prey. Plus, its mouth is lined with sharp spikes called dermal denticles. Scientists believe it may be able to eat prey half the size of its body. It mostly feasts on squid, but it has been known to cannibalize other sharks. In the shark world, it's often eat or get eaten.

HABITAT

Deep waters worldwide, including the Arctic Sea, the Mediterranean Sea, and the Pacific Ocean

SHARK STATS

6.4 ft.

LENGTH: Up to 6.4 ft. (2 m)
WEIGHT: Unknown

FEAR FACTOR

1

Because it lives so deep in the water, it seldom poses a threat to humans.

FREAKY FACT

This prehistoric-looking fish is a ghost of the sea, remaining unseen in its natural habitat until 2004. It's the suspect behind age-old sea serpent sightings.

DISTINCTIVE FEATURE

The frilled shark gets its name from its frilled gills. With its eel-like body, this shark winds and twists like a snake as it swims.

GOBLIN SHARK

MITSUKURINA OWSTONI

BE VERY AFRAID

The flabby-bodied, pinkish-gray goblin shark looks creepy, but would-be prey assumes it's no threat as it moves very slowly along the ocean's bottom. But then, as its body remains still, it pops out its jaws and traps fish, crabs, and cephalopods in its bristle-like fangs. It finds its prey using electroreception, which allows it to sense the electrical fields of other creatures deep underwater. This is important in the dark ocean depths. Because of its dark environment, the goblin shark has very small eyes, an adaptation because of its limited need for sight and its resulting reliance on other senses.

HABITAT
Deep waters in the Atlantic and Pacific Oceans, the Gulf of Mexico, and the Indian Ocean

SHARK STATS

12.6 ft.

LENGTH: 8.7 to 12.6 ft. (2.7 to 3.8 m)
WEIGHT: Up to 463 lbs. (210 kg)

FREAKY FACT
Named for a Japanese demon, the spooky-looking goblin shark inspired the design of a monster in the 2017 movie *Alien: Covenant*.

FEAR FACTOR
2

This deep-water shark seldom poses a threat to humans— but it could!

DISTINCTIVE FEATURE

This cousin of the frilled shark can shoot its jaw out of its face like an alien when prey is nearby. This shark's massive, quick-extending jaw can open at a 111-degree angle, allowing it to ambush and immediately swallow prey.

GALAPAGOS SHARK

CARCHARHINUS GALAPAGENSIS

LEAN, MEAN KILLING MACHINES

Galapagos sharks have the unfortunate combination of bad attitude, speed, and power that makes them creatures to avoid. They're sensitive to vibrations and the electrical fields of potential prey, which can include other sharks, even—gasp!—their own young. These curious animals live closer to the surface as they grow older, making them more of a threat to people. They are, in fact, considered more dangerous than hammerheads. They become even more aggressive when fishers try to chase them away, sometimes sending them into an attack frenzy that can last way too long for comfort. Like other shark species, they are hunted for their fins, which are used in shark fin soup.

HABITAT

The warmer waters of the Atlantic, Pacific, and Indian Oceans

SHARK STATS

12.2 ft.

LENGTH: 9 ft. 10 in. to 12 ft. 2 in. (3 to 3.7 m)
WEIGHT: Up to 330.7 lbs. (150 kg)

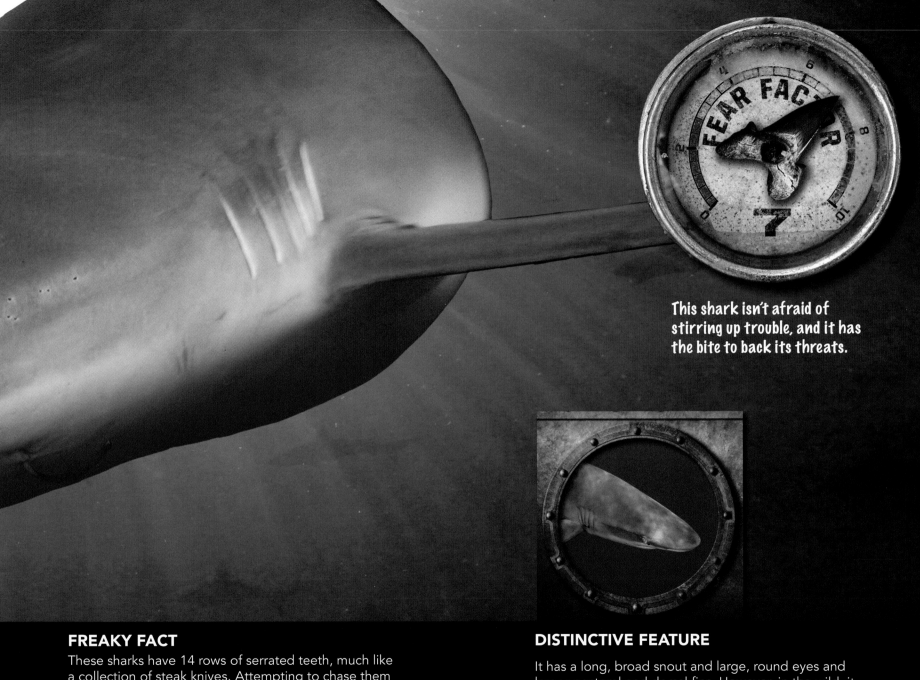

FEAR FACTOR

7

This shark isn't afraid of stirring up trouble, and it has the bite to back its threats.

FREAKY FACT

These sharks have 14 rows of serrated teeth, much like a collection of steak knives. Attempting to chase them away only gets them angry, provoking them to attack anything within reach.

DISTINCTIVE FEATURE

It has a long, broad snout and large, round eyes and larger pectoral and dorsal fins. However, in the wild, it is easily confused with other requiem sharks, the family of large and dangerous sharks to which it belongs.

SHORTFIN MAKO SHARK

ISURUS OXYRINCHUS

FAST AND FURIOUS

Valued for its meat, this shark is more threatened by humans than humans are by it. But that doesn't change the fact it's often ranked among the top 12 most dangerous sharks. Every animal around it is considered fair game. Makos even eat one another as they develop during pregnancy. They're also world travelers, able to travel far as well as fast. They have been known to travel nearly 1,305 mi. (2,100 km) in just more than a month. But surfers beware: Young sharks, known as pups, like to hang out in the warm waters off the coast of San Diego, California.

HABITAT

Pacific Ocean, especially near the Western United States; Atlantic Ocean, the Gulf of Mexico

SHARK STATS

7 ft.

LENGTH: Up to 7 ft. (2.1 m)
WEIGHT: Up to 1,113 lbs. (505 kg)

Shortfin makos are often caught for food but can be deadly to fishermen.

FREAKY FACT

The torpedo-shaped body of the shortfin mako makes it the world's fastest shark, clocking speeds as high as 43 mph (70 kph). Shortfin makos can also leap 20 to 30 ft. (6.1 to 9.1 m) out of the water and have been known to jump into fishing boats.

DISTINCTIVE FEATURE

The teeth of these apex predators—cousins of the infamous great white shark—stick out even when their mouths are closed. They're also noted for being warm-blooded, which helps them better endure cooler water.

SICKLEFIN LEMON SHARK

NEGAPRION ACUTIDENS

PREDATOR AND PREY

Sicklefin lemon sharks tend to live in shallower waters, often near the shoreline. Their dorsal fins are often seen above the water. Because they're so easy to find, they're also easy to hunt for their meat and fins, used in shark fin soup. This has reduced their population. But fishermen have learned to tread carefully with this shark. Given the chance, this naturally shy shark will fight back. No one wants to be on the receiving end of that fight, especially with a shark that has large, serrated teeth!

HABITAT

Shallower waters of the Pacific and Atlantic Oceans, the Indian Ocean, and the Red Sea

SHARK STATS

LENGTH: Up to 14 ft. (4.3 m)
WEIGHT: Up to 397 lbs. (150 kg)

14 ft.

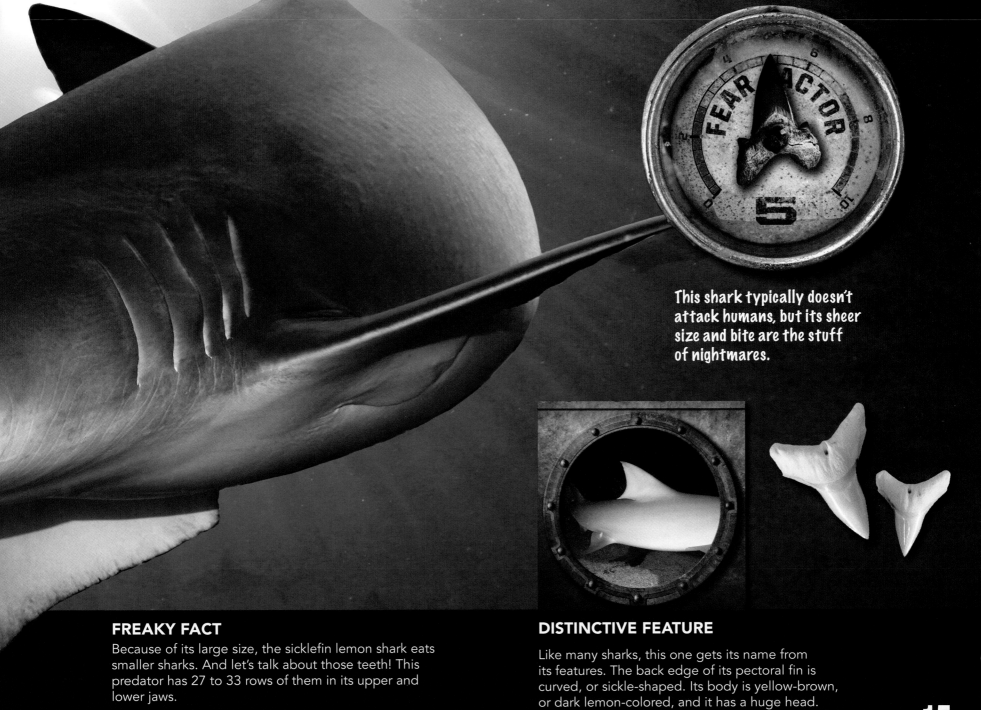

FEAR FACTOR 5

This shark typically doesn't attack humans, but its sheer size and bite are the stuff of nightmares.

FREAKY FACT

Because of its large size, the sicklefin lemon shark eats smaller sharks. And let's talk about those teeth! This predator has 27 to 33 rows of them in its upper and lower jaws.

DISTINCTIVE FEATURE

Like many sharks, this one gets its name from its features. The back edge of its pectoral fin is curved, or sickle-shaped. Its body is yellow-brown, or dark lemon-colored, and it has a huge head.

LEMON SHARK

NEGAPRION BREVIROSTRIS

STRENGTH IN NUMBERS

The lemon shark enjoys being part of a community. It likes to hang out with a large group of its predatory, cannibalistic friends. Living in a group promotes mating and helps lemon sharks protect their young against predators. They also learn from each other. This behavior makes them unusual among sharks. But that's not the only behavior that sets them apart. They're also known to rest on the ocean bottom during the day. Believe it or not, that's hard work for a shark, which must pump water through its gills to keep from sinking. That happens naturally when it swims.

HABITAT
Coastal waters of the North Pacific Ocean, Atlantic Ocean, and the Gulf of Mexico

SHARK STATS

11.10 ft.

LENGTH: 7 ft. 10 in. to 11 ft. 10 in. (2.4 to 3.6 m)
WEIGHT: 198.4 to 403.4 lbs (90 to 183 kg)

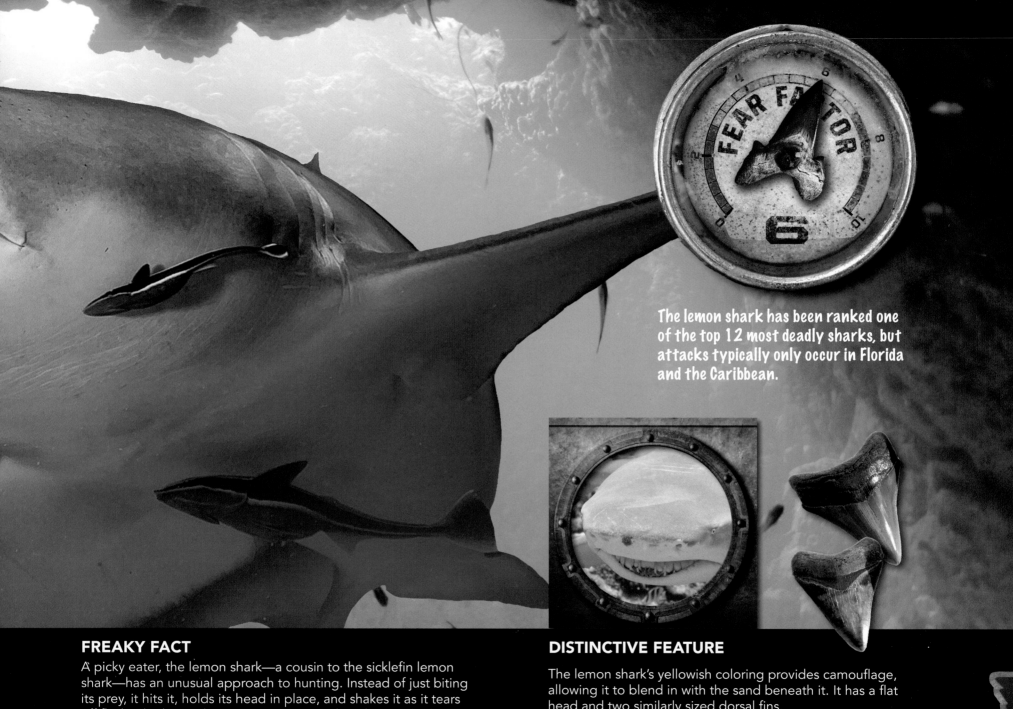

The lemon shark has been ranked one of the top 12 most deadly sharks, but attacks typically only occur in Florida and the Caribbean.

FREAKY FACT

A picky eater, the lemon shark—a cousin to the sicklefin lemon shark—has an unusual approach to hunting. Instead of just biting its prey, it hits it, holds its head in place, and shakes it as it tears off flesh. The lesson here: Don't get eaten by a lemon shark.

DISTINCTIVE FEATURE

The lemon shark's yellowish coloring provides camouflage, allowing it to blend in with the sand beneath it. It has a flat head and two similarly sized dorsal fins.

GREAT HAMMERHEAD SHARK

SPHYRNA MOKARRAN

BE VERY AFRAID

The great hammerhead has three fearsome qualities: its huge size, its bite, and its unpredictable nature. Research from the University of Tampa in Florida found the great hammerhead is among the most ferocious shark species. It has been blamed for 17 unprovoked attacks on humans, none of which have been fatal. The good news is that the great hammerhead typically eats fish, stingrays, and invertebrates. Like many other sharks, it also is cannibalistic. But the predator often becomes prey to humans, who hunt it for its fins, hides, and liver oil, which is used in vitamins.

HABITAT

Largely found in coastal areas of the Atlantic and Pacific Oceans, the Gulf of Mexico, and the Mediterranean Sea

SHARK STATS

20 ft.

LENGTH: 13 to 20 ft. (4 to 6 m)
WEIGHT: 500 to 1,000 lbs. (226.8 to 453.6 kg)

Though it seldom attacks humans, the hammerhead will not hesitate to defend itself if it's provoked. And with its size and bite force, it's very capable of defending itself.

FREAKY FACT

Though it has attacked humans only 17 times and never fatally, the hammerhead is considered one of the top 10 most deadly sharks. It ranks just below great whites and tiger sharks in biting power and number of attacks.

DISTINCTIVE FEATURE

This odd-looking shark gets its name for its mallet-shaped head. Because of its head shape, the hammerhead's eyes are wide set, allowing it a broad field of vision for identifying prey. It also has increased sensitivity to the electrical fields of nearby sea creatures.

BLACKTIP REEF SHARK

CARCHARHINUS MELANOPTERUS

A SHARK AMBASSADOR

The blacktip reef shark is a frequent draw to divers who want to encounter a "safer" shark in the wild, making it valuable in the tourism industry. However, it has been known to bite swimmers or waders, though not fatally. Commonly found in coral reefs, the blacktip reef shark feeds on octopuses, squid, crabs, lobsters, shrimp, snakes, and reef fish. It also is often found in aquariums because of its hardiness and small size. Its size makes it less popular than other shark species among commercial fishers, though sometimes it is caught for its fins, meat, and liver oil, which is used in vitamins.

HABITAT

Shallow waters in the Pacific Ocean and the Red and Mediterranean Seas

SHARK STATS

5.9 ft.

LENGTH: Up to 5.9 ft. (1.6 m)
WEIGHT: Up to 30 lbs. (13.6 kg)

FEAR FACTOR 4

The blacktip reef shark can become aggressive around spear fishing. They have also been known to bite people in shallow waters, though such attacks are rare.

FREAKY FACT

Don't think you can avoid the blacktip reef shark if you stay out of the ocean. It is also found in brackish and fresh water.

DISTINCTIVE FEATURE

This smaller shark, not to be confused with the blacktip shark, has black-tipped fins with white highlights. Its lower teeth are serrated like steak knives.

BLACKTIP SHARK

CARCHARHINUS LIMBATUS

TOO CLOSE FOR COMFORT

The menacing blacktip shark likes to live and raise its young in shallow coastal waters, where it can protect pups from larger sharks. But this puts it in frequent contact with humans, occasionally causing it to mistake a swimmer for prey. A University of Tampa study ranked the blacktip shark as one of the five most fierce shark species. This powerful shark is also known to leap out of the water, spin, and splash down on its back. It sometimes uses this technique to attack schools of fish just below the surface. Like other sharks, the blacktip is sometimes hunted for its fins and hide.

HABITAT
Coastal waters in the Atlantic and Pacific Oceans, the Gulf of Mexico, and the Caribbean and Mediterranean Seas

SHARK STATS

8 ft.

LENGTH: Up to 8 ft. (2.4 m)
WEIGHT: 66 to 220 lbs. (29.9 to 99.8 kg)

FEAR FACTOR

If you're swimming or surfing in Florida waters, this is the shark you're most likely to encounter. Good news: Its bites seldom result in death.

FREAKY FACT

Ranked as the fourth most deadly shark species with 29 attacks to its credit, the blacktip shark is the culprit behind 20 percent of all shark attacks in Florida. Surfers, beware!

DISTINCTIVE FEATURE

Like the blacktip reef shark, the blacktip shark has black-tipped fins. However, it's much larger and meaner than the blacktip reef shark.

BLUE SHARK

PRIONACE GLAUCA

IT'S EVERYWHERE

A cousin of the much-feared bull shark (see pp. 36-37), the blue shark is the world's most widely distributed shark. It's also one of the fastest sharks clocking speeds up to 25 mph (40 kph). Like many other shark species, it cannibalizes other sharks, and it sometimes hunts in packs. It's also the most widely fished shark. Between 10 million and 20 million are killed each year. Many get caught in fishing nets, and others are hunted for their fins, which are used in shark fin soup. They are also prey to killer whales and larger sharks.

HABITAT

Cooler waters in the open ocean worldwide; deeper waters in the tropics

SHARK STATS

13 ft.

LENGTH: 12.6 ft. to 13 ft. (3.8 to 4 m)
WEIGHT: About 529 lbs. (240 kg)

FEAR FACTOR
6

If your plane crashes into the ocean or you're shipwrecked, beware that pretty blue shark circling you.

FREAKY FACT

Though this shark isn't typically aggressive toward humans, it's been known to attack people who have been lost at sea. Sometimes it just likes to sample a bite of an arm or leg.

DISTINCTIVE FEATURE

You can spot this shark by its indigo blue coloring and its slender, aerodynamic body. Females are typically larger than males and are also noted by bite marks they receive during mating.

DUSKY SHARK

CARCHARHINUS OBSCURUS

A WANDERER

The dusky shark is migratory, traveling up to 2,000 mi. (3,218.7 km) seasonally to find water that's just the right temperature. In the summer, it travels toward either pole. Come winter, it returns to the Equator. Female dusky sharks always give birth where they themselves were born, but this can cause overfishing for their meat and fins. If left alone by human or marine predators, such as bull sharks, a dusky shark can live up to 50 years. Smaller sharks are less long-lived if they encounter a dusky shark, however.

HABITAT

Shallow coastal waters to depths of 1,300 ft. (396.2 m) in the Atlantic and Pacific Oceans

SHARK STATS

13 ft.

LENGTH: 11.8 to 13 ft. (3.6 to 4 m)
WEIGHT: 350 to 400 lbs. (158.8 to 181.4 kg)

FEAR FACTOR 4

The dusky shark is typically not a threat to humans except when it ventures near the shore. But its size and serrated upper and lower teeth make it potentially dangerous to people.

FREAKY FACT

This shark has a powerful bite force with 13 to 15 rows of serrated teeth. It sets up nurseries in coastal waters to avoid predators, putting itself—as well as surfers and swimmers—at risk.

DISTINCTIVE FEATURE

Often mistaken for the Galapagos shark, a fellow member of the requiem family, the dusky shark is noted for its bluish-gray upper body, white underside, and long pectoral fin.

NURSE SHARK

GINGLYMOSTOMA CIRRATUM

DON'T ASK FOR THE NURSE

You would think a creature with "nurse" in its name would be friendly and helpful. Not this nurse. It doesn't attack people often, but when it does, its powerful suction and grip make it difficult to get free. This shark generally rests during the day and hunts at night, when its prey—such as large-shelled creatures, which it sucks and chews out of their homes—is probably resting. Like lemon sharks, nurse sharks are sometimes found in large groups, sometimes even lying on top of each other. Also like other sharks, they're an important part of their ecosystem—in this case, coral reefs.

HABITAT
Shallow waters of the Atlantic and Pacific Oceans

SHARK STATS

9.75 ft.

LENGTH: 7.5 to 9.75 ft. (2.3 to 3 m)
WEIGHT: 200 to 330 lbs. (90.7 to 149.7 kg)

The frequency of attacks is increasing as tourists feed nurse sharks in the wild. The moral of the story: Don't feed sharks.

FREAKY FACT

Despite its small mouth and friendly-sounding name, the nurse shark has such a powerful bite that rescuers have had to use surgical tools to free victims from its jaws.

DISTINCTIVE FEATURE

The nurse shark makes a sucking sound like a nursing baby when hunting, which may explain the origin of its name. Its scientific name means "curled, hinged mouth," a fitting description of its jaws.

BROADNOSE SEVENGILL SHARK

NOTORYNCHUS CEPEDIANUS

WHEN OPPORTUNITY STRIKES

With its sharp, serrated teeth, the broadnose sevengill is both a fierce hunter and a scavenger. It seems to move slowly—that is, until it goes after prey. Then it shoots forward in a burst of speed. It eats seals and other marine mammals, rays, and carcasses, including human carcasses. It sometimes ambushes or sneaks up on prey, including in a pack. It can swim in very shallow water, and it will attack if provoked, increasing its threat level to humans. However, it sometimes becomes prey to great whites, and it is sometimes hunted for its hide and liver oil.

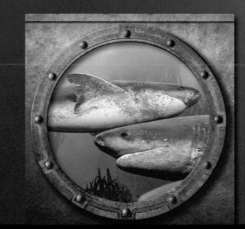

HABITAT

Coastal waters less than 164 ft. (50 m) deep in parts of the Atlantic and Pacific Oceans and the Mediterranean Sea

SHARK STATS

9.8 ft.

LENGTH: Up to 9.8 ft. (3 m)
WEIGHT: Up to 236 lbs. (107 kg)

FEAR FACTOR 7

The broadnose sevengill is an opportunistic eater and can be dangerous to humans.

FREAKY FACT

The broadnose sevengill shark hunts at night, so much of its behavior is a mystery to researchers. But they do know this shark is a powerful apex predator that hunts in packs, often feasts on other sharks, and shares hunting grounds with great whites.

DISTINCTIVE FEATURE

Also known as the cow shark, the broadnose sevengill is named for its broad nose and seven gills, a contrast to the five gills found in most sharks. Its dorsal fin is so far back on its body that it may appear to be missing.

BRONZE WHALER SHARK

CARCHARHINUS BRACHYURUS

AN EATING MACHINE

Also known as a copper shark, the bronze whaler is an intelligent and effective hunter that largely eats squid, octopuses, rays, and fish. A single shark can eat millions of sardines. Its coloring provides camouflage from predators and prey. Young bronze whalers may get eaten by larger sharks, but adults return the favor by eating smaller sharks. This aggressive predator sometimes hunts in groups, also relying on them when mating and migrating. It has been known to migrate up to 808 mi. (1,300 km) to find a mate, food, or water that's the right temperature.

HABITAT

In shallow bays and deeper waters in the Atlantic Ocean, the Pacific Ocean near the Indian Sea, the Mediterranean Sea, and the Gulf of Mexico

SHARK STATS

11.5 ft.

LENGTH: Usually up to 9.8 ft. (3 m), with some growing to 11.5 ft. (3.5 m)
WEIGHT: Up to 672.4 lbs. (305 kg)

FEAR FACTOR 5

Unless you're a spearfisher or you're swimming in its habitat around a school of fish, you have little to fear from a bronze whaler.

FREAKY FACT

This shark has been blamed in 15 attacks on people since 1962, with one death to its credit. Its most frequent attacks are on spearfishers. It is especially dangerous around food sources.

DISTINCTIVE FEATURE

A type of requiem shark sometimes confused with the dusky shark, the bronze whaler has a bronze-colored line of raised skin between its dorsal fins, and it has hook-shaped upper teeth.

GREAT WHITE SHARK

CARCHARODON CARCHARIAS

THE GREATEST JAWS OF ALL

The great white shark might not have inspired the book and movie *Jaws* (read about bull sharks on pp. 36-37), but it deserves its bad reputation. It's responsible for at least 80 fatal unprovoked attacks and 314 total attacks. Some scientists think man-eating is a rookie mistake for young great whites. The young sharks may mistake surfers for seals, a favorite item on the great white shark's menu. Great whites typically take a sample bite, but with the great white's teeth and jaws, even a sample bite can prove deadly from blood loss or damage to organs. These fast, powerful swimmers can breach out of the water, making for a great show—from a safe distance.

HABITAT

From the surf line to depths of as much as 4,265 ft. (1,300 m) in the Atlantic and Pacific Oceans, the Gulf of Mexico, the Indian Ocean, and the Mediterranean Sea

SHARK STATS

20 ft.

LENGTH: Up to 20 ft. (6.1 m)
WEIGHT: Up to 2.5 tons (2.3 tonnes)

If ever there were a shark to fear, this is the one. It's big, it's bad, and it has the massive jaws and saw-like teeth to prove it.

FREAKY FACT

Measuring about half the length of a school bus, the great white is the world's largest predatory fish and is responsible for up to half of all shark bites worldwide.

DISTINCTIVE FEATURE

You can spot this apex predator by its massive size, its torpedo shape, its gray back and white belly, and its 300 triangular teeth. Let's hope you never get close enough to count them.

BULL SHARK

CARCHARHINUS LEUCAS

DESERVING THE SPOTLIGHT

In 1916, a bull shark attacked five New Jersey beachgoers, killing four. The attacks inspired the book *Jaws*, which was turned into a movie by the same name in 1975. However, in both, a great white shark was credited for the attacks. The bull shark is especially dangerous because it likes to live in populated areas, and it can be found in fresh water as well as salt water. Like other sharks, it eats smaller sharks, but the bull shark will even eat other bull sharks. This fearless predator has even been known to eat hippos, considered the world's deadliest land animal.

HABITAT

Coastal areas in depths up to 492 ft. (150 m) in the Atlantic and Indian Oceans

SHARK STATS

13.1 ft.

LENGTH: Up to 13.1 ft. (4 m)
WEIGHT: Up to 697.8 lbs. (316.5 kg)

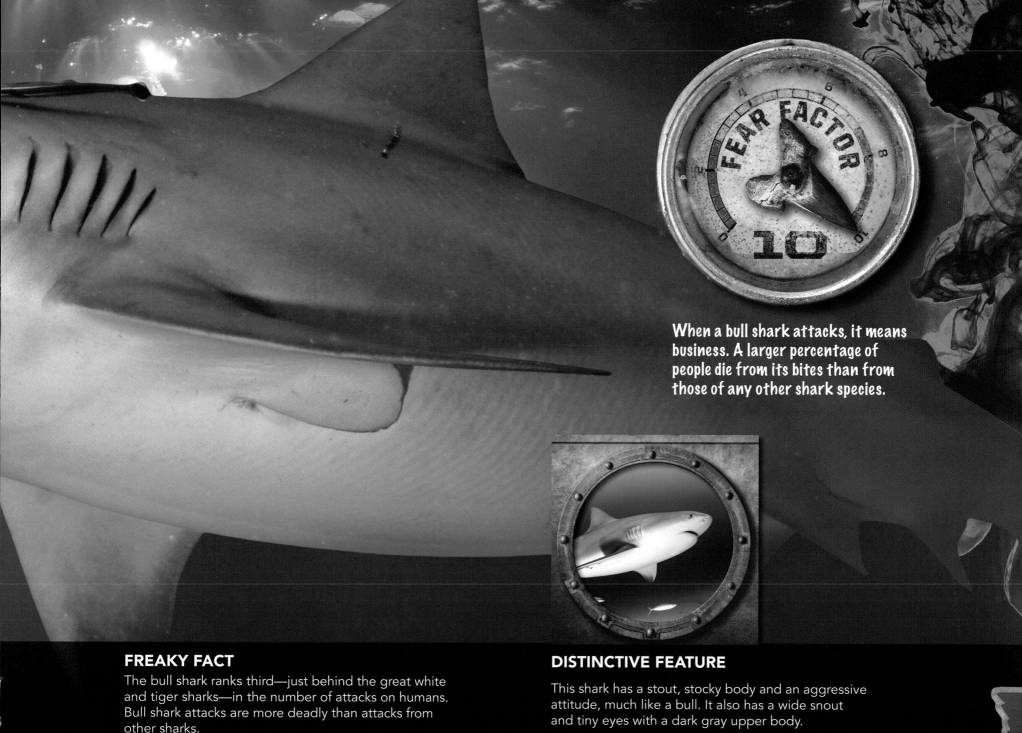

FEAR FACTOR

10

When a bull shark attacks, it means business. A larger percentage of people die from its bites than from those of any other shark species.

FREAKY FACT

The bull shark ranks third—just behind the great white and tiger sharks—in the number of attacks on humans. Bull shark attacks are more deadly than attacks from other sharks.

DISTINCTIVE FEATURE

This shark has a stout, stocky body and an aggressive attitude, much like a bull. It also has a wide snout and tiny eyes with a dark gray upper body.

SAND TIGER SHARK

CARCHARIAS TAURUS

A TAME (NON) TIGER

The sand tiger may not be a true tiger shark, but it is a cousin to the great white. However, this cousin must come from the nicer side of the family because it has been blamed for only 29 unprovoked attacks on people since 1580, none of them deadly. Regardless, the sand tiger shark is a large, intelligent predator. Hunting begins early: While developing inside its mother, the larger pup will eat its smaller siblings. This shark has been seen hunting in groups, cracking its tail like a bullwhip to round up a school of yellow kingfish. It also is often seen lingering around shipwrecks.

HABITAT

Along shorelines in oceans worldwide except for the eastern Pacific. Also found in the Mediterranean Sea.

SHARK STATS

10 ft.

LENGTH: Up to 10 ft. (3 m)
WEIGHT: Up to 400 lbs. (181.4 kg)

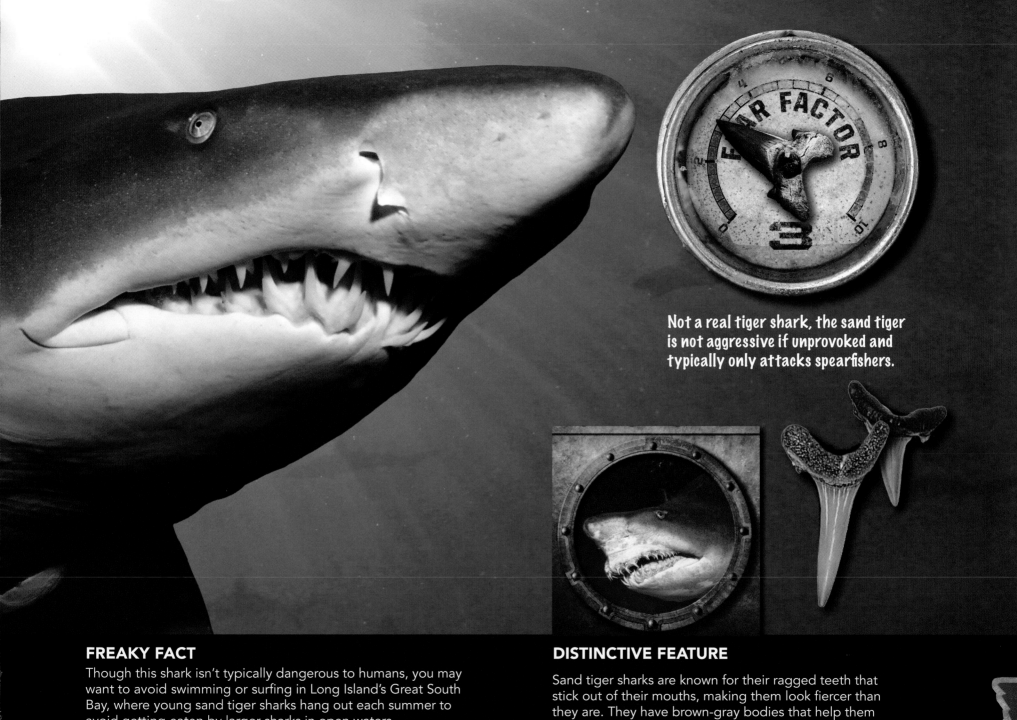

Not a real tiger shark, the sand tiger is not aggressive if unprovoked and typically only attacks spearfishers.

FREAKY FACT

Though this shark isn't typically dangerous to humans, you may want to avoid swimming or surfing in Long Island's Great South Bay, where young sand tiger sharks hang out each summer to avoid getting eaten by larger sharks in open waters.

DISTINCTIVE FEATURE

Sand tiger sharks are known for their ragged teeth that stick out of their mouths, making them look fiercer than they are. They have brown-gray bodies that help them blend in with the sand below, earning them their name.

TIGER SHARK

GALEOCERDO CUVIER

SURF WITH CAUTION

In 2003, a tiger shark ripped off the arm of 13-year-old competitive surfer Bethany Hamilton, inspiring the 2011 movie *Soul Surfer*. The apex predator is often found in the waters of Hawaii, Hamilton's home, and has sometimes been hunted to reduce the number of attacks on tourists. The plan never worked because the remaining tiger sharks simply stepped up their game. The tiger shark, the bull shark, and the great white shark make up what's called "The Big Three," the sharks most likely to attack humans. The tiger shark's saw-like teeth can rip through pretty much anything, including the shells of sea turtles.

HABITAT

In warmer, murky coastal waters worldwide (except for the Mediterranean Sea) at depths from 20 ft. (6.1 m) to 3,000 ft. (914.4 m)

SHARK STATS

16 ft.

LENGTH: Up to 16 ft. (4.9 m)
WEIGHT: Up to 1,800 lbs. (816.5 kg)

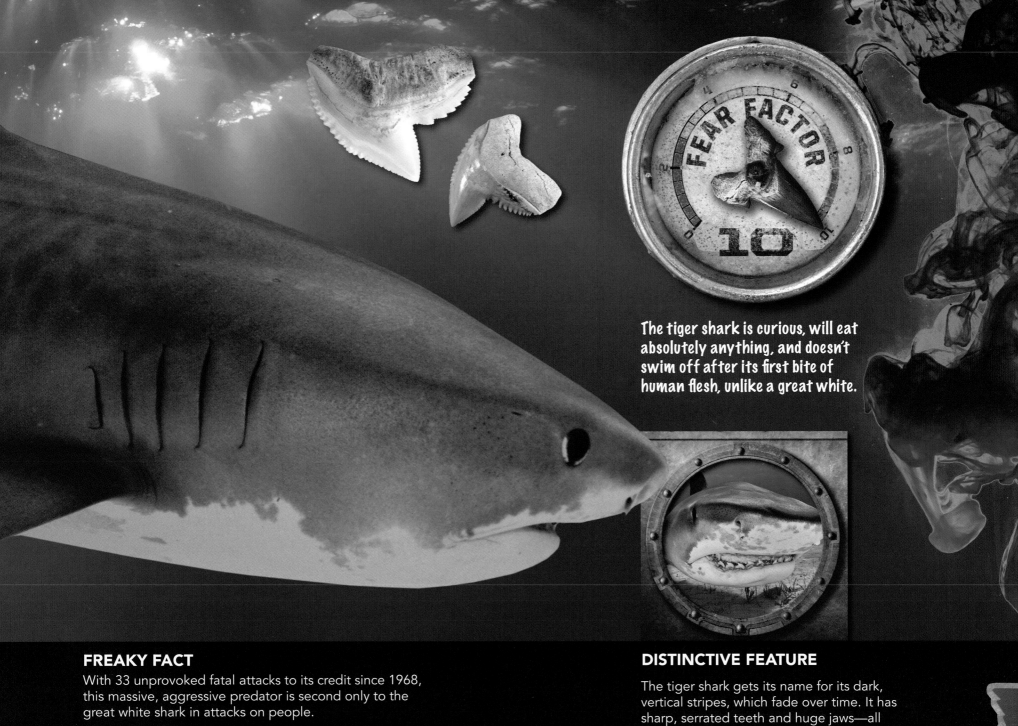

FEAR FACTOR 10

The tiger shark is curious, will eat absolutely anything, and doesn't swim off after its first bite of human flesh, unlike a great white.

FREAKY FACT

With 33 unprovoked fatal attacks to its credit since 1968, this massive, aggressive predator is second only to the great white shark in attacks on people.

DISTINCTIVE FEATURE

The tiger shark gets its name for its dark, vertical stripes, which fade over time. It has sharp, serrated teeth and huge jaws—all the better for eating you with, my dear.

SPINNER SHARK

CARCHARHINUS BREVIPINNA

A NATURAL ACROBAT

This slender-bodied shark snaps its narrow jaws in every direction as it quickly swims through a school of fish and breaches the surface at full speed in its trademark aerial spin. It hunts in groups and raises its young along shorelines in the summer, which can be a concern for people in coastal areas. Although this shark may attack people, its narrow jaws and small teeth are unlikely to do serious harm. It mostly feeds on various fish, stingrays, octopuses, and squid. It also has been seen scavenging fish from fishing boats. Younger spinner sharks can fall prey to larger sharks.

HABITAT

Shallow coastal waters in parts of the Atlantic, Pacific, and Indian Oceans, and the Mediterranean Sea

SHARK STATS

6.4 ft.

LENGTH: An average of 6.4 ft. (1.95 m)
WEIGHT: About 123 lbs. (55.8 kg)

FEAR FACTOR 4

Spinner sharks like to hunt schools of fish, so if you're spearfishing or diving near a school, watch out.

FREAKY FACT

In bad news, this species has attacked humans without cause 16 times. In good news, it hasn't killed anyone.

DISTINCTIVE FEATURE

Similar in appearance to a blacktip shark (though larger), it has a black-tipped anal fin, giving it one more black-tipped fin than the blacktip. Spinner sharks are easier to spot above the water, where they will spin up to 20 ft. (6.1 m) in the air.

OCEANIC WHITETIP SHARK

CARCHARHINUS LONGIMANUS

WHEN OPPORTUNITY STRIKES

The oceanic whitetip shark makes the most of every opportunity. When a plane or ship sinks into the ocean, count on this predator making itself known. As one of the most abundant large fish found in the ocean, it's likely to be nearby where waters are deep. Famous French oceanographer Jacques Cousteau ranked this shark as one of the most dangerous in the ocean for good reason. Most sharks will retreat when divers jab them in the snout. Not the oceanic whitetip: It just gets more curious and bolder. It typically eats large fish such as tuna, and other shark species will yield to it at feeding sites.

HABITAT

Generally found in warmer upper layers of the open ocean in the Atlantic and Pacific Oceans and the Mediterranean and Red Seas

SHARK STATS

13 ft.

LENGTH: Up to 13 ft. (4 m)
WEIGHT: Up to 370 lbs. (167.8 kg)

FEAR FACTOR

10

These large, aggressive, unpredictable predators show little fear of humans.

FREAKY FACT

During World War II, the oceanic whitetip was blamed for the deaths of 150 crew members of the downed *USS Indianapolis* and as many as 800 crew members of the downed British ship Nova Scotia.

DISTINCTIVE FEATURE

The oceanic whitetip shark can be identified by its white-tipped fins. Its dorsal fin is large and rounded, and its pectoral fin is shaped like a paddle.

SAVE THE SHARKS

EVEN SCARY CREATURES HAVE THEIR PLACE

Sharks are the apex predator of our oceans. They are powerful, terrifying, and deadly. But they're also important. Without them, the ocean's food chain would be out of balance.

Sharks may reign above most ocean predators, but they fall prey to an even more powerful and deadly predator: humans. People enjoy shark meat and shark fin soup. They enjoy shark liver oil as supplements. Their appetite for sharks comes at a huge price. An estimated three sharks are killed every second.

Some sharks are hunted just for their jaws, which are used as trophies. Some are accidentally caught in fishing lines, their bodies discarded by fishermen. Some are poisoned by sewage, chemicals, and garbage. As a result, some species, such as dusky sharks, are quickly disappearing.

You can help by sharing what you've learned about sharks by:

- Avoiding shark products
- Reusing and recycling
- Picking up garbage along the beaches

Let's work together to protect these amazing (and fearsome!) creatures and the oceans they inhabit. Even scary creatures deserve our respect!

The shark teeth included in this book are fossils from the sand tiger and corax sharks. They are found in the phosphate plateau of Khouribga, Morocco. An immense amount of marine fossils are found in the phosphate mines. The teeth in your hands are from creatures from a time long, long ago. The sand tiger is still around today, but not the corax (also called the squalicorax shark.) The corax lived 105-65 million years ago. The corax shark tooth is serrated like teeth of the tiger shark.